BASKETBALL LEGENDS

Kareem Abdul-Jabbar

Charles Barkley

Larry Bird

Wilt Chamberlain

Clyde Drexler

Julius Erving

Patrick Ewing

Anfernee Hardaway

Grant Hill

Magic Johnson

Michael Jordan

Jason Kidd

Reggie Miller

Hakeem Olajuwon

Shaquille O'Neal

Scottie Pippen

David Robinson

Dennis Rodman

CHELSEA HOUSE PUBLISHERS

GRANT HILL

Daniel Bial

Introduction by
Chuck Daly

CHELSEA HOUSE PUBLISHERS
New York   Philadelphia

Produced by Daniel Bial and Associates
New York, New York

Picture research by Alan Gottlieb
Cover illustration by Bill Vann

3 5 7 9 8 6 4

Library of Congress Cataloging-in-Publication Data

Bial, Daniel, 1955-
     Grant Hill / Daniel Bial ; introduction by Chuck Daly.
          p.   cm. -- (Basketball legends)
     Includes bibliographical references (p.) and index.
     Summary: The life story of the first NBA rookie ever to become the leading
     vote-getter for an All-Star game.
     ISBN 0-7910-2436-9 (lib. bdg.)
     1. Hill, Grant--Juvenile literature. 2. Basketball players--United States--
     Biography--Juvenile literature. [1. Hill, Grant. 2. Basketball players.
     3. Afro-Americans--Biography.] I. Title. II. Series.
     GV884.H45853 1996
     796.323'092--dc20
     [B]
                                                              96-10678
                                                                 CIP
                                                                  AC

CONTENTS

BECOMING A
BASKETBALL LEGEND

Chuck Daly

What does it take to be a basketball superstar? Two of the three things it takes are easy to spot. Any great athlete must have excellent skills and tremendous dedication. The third quality needed is much harder to define, or even put in words. Others call it leadership or desire to win, but I'm not sure that explains it fully. This third quality relates to the athlete's thinking process, a certain mentality and work ethic. One can coach athletic skills, and while few superstars need outside influence to help keep them dedicated, it is possible for a coach to offer some well-timed words in order to keep that athlete fully motivated. But a coach can do no more than appeal to a player's will to win; how much that player is then capable of ensuring victory is up to his own internal workings.

In recent times, we have been fortunate to have seen some of the best to play the game. Larry Bird, Magic Johnson, and Michael Jordan had all three components of superstardom in full measure. They brought their teams to numerous championships, and made the players around them better. (They also made their coaches look smart.)

I myself coached a player who belongs in that class, Isiah Thomas, who helped lead the Detroit Pistons to consecutive NBA crowns. Isiah is not tall-he's just over six feet-but he could do whatever he wanted with the ball. And what he wanted to do most was lead and win.

All the players I mentioned above and those whom this series will chronicle are tremendously gifted athletes, but for the most part, you can't play professional basketball at all unless you have excellent skills. And few players get to stay on their team unless they are willing to dedicate themselves to improving their talents even more, learning about their opponents, and finding a way to join with their teammates and win.

It's that third element that separates the good player from the superstar, the memorable players from the legends of the game. Superstars know when to take over the game. If the situation calls for a defensive stop, the superstars stand up and do it. If the situation calls for a key pass, they make it. And if the situation calls for a big shot, they want the ball. They don't want the ball simply because of their own glory or ego. Instead they know—and their teammates know—that they are the ones who can deliver, regardless of the pressure.

The words "legend" and "superstar" are often tossed around without real meaning. Taking a hard look at some of those who truly can be classified as "legends" can provide insight into the things that brought them to that level. All of them developed their legacy over numerous seasons of play, even if certain games will always stand out in the memories of those who saw them. Those games typically featured amazing feats of all-around play. No matter how great the fans thought the superstars were, these players were capable of surprising the fans, their opponents, and occasionally even themselves. The desire to win took over, and with their dedication and athletic skills already in place, they were capable of the most astonishing achievements.

CHUCK DALY, most recently the head coach of the New Jersey Nets, guided the Detroit Pistons to two straight NBA championships, in 1989 and 1990. He earned a gold medal as coach of the 1992 U.S. Olympic basketball team—the so-called "Dream Team"—and was inducted into the Pro Basketball Hall of Fame in 1994.

1

MOST WANTED TO SUCCEED

In 1995, the leading vote-getter for the National Basketball Association (NBA) All-Star game was a rookie—someone who had played in the league for only half a season in his entire career. No one had ever done this before. Larry Bird, Magic Johnson, and Michael Jordan had all been terrific players when they first turned pro but they had not come close to being the lead vote-getter for the All-Star Game.

Perhaps the most amazing thing about Grant Hill's receiving nearly one million three hundred thousand votes in the 1995 All-Star balloting was that he was not even having a tremendous season. Playing for the Detroit Pistons, he was averaging 18 points, 4 assists, and 5 rebounds per game—fine numbers, but there were at least ten other players with superior statistics. So why did the fans bestow this rare honor on him?

The simple reason for his popularity was: the

Grant Hill has Charles Barkley looking the wrong way as he goes in for a slam dunk in the 1995 All-Star Game.

fans *liked* Grant Hill. "Hill exudes 'regular guy,'" said Brian Murphy, editor of the *Sports Marketing Letter*. "You admire him, but you feel you could talk to him if you met him."

"This has been a very sour year in sports, with player contract squabbles and the baseball and hockey strikes," pointed out Nova Lanktree, owner of Lanktree Sports Celebrity Network. "People look at Grant Hill, with his charisma and all his solidness and all his excitement, and they think, 'Hey, maybe we do have a hero here.'"

Other basketball stars seemed to be doing all they could to make the public not like them. If you looked at who showed up at the All-Star Game, you can easily see why a pleasant young star such as Grant Hill would be a breath of fresh air. Charles Barkley had long been famous for outrageous comments; recently he had spat on a young girl sitting at court side. When Shaquille O'Neal had a Superman "S" tattooed on his arm he was basically telling the world that he felt superior to everyone. Karl Malone and Patrick Ewing had reputations as whiners when things did not go their way. Roy Tarpley had been suspended from the league for drug use. Dennis Rodman was a fine defensive player and terrific rebounder, but he had recently garnered headlines for his full-body-covering tattoos, green- or purple-dyed hair, I-don't-give-a-damn attitude, and team disciplinary problems. Rodman had been a charter member of the "Bad Boys," the championship Pistons team that was famous for their hard fouls, trash talk, and arrogance. After being traded to the San Antonio Spurs, he had seemingly gone out of his way to alienate fans.

Joe Dumars, a teammate of Grant Hill's on the Detroit Pistons, said, "It's a league of guys who are out of control. Fringe behavior is being rec-

ognized and accepted, sometimes even rewarded. It's probably not a healthy comment that
Grant is being recognized for just being a good
person, but it's time we get back to that."

The first two people chosen in the 1995 draft,
Glenn Robinson and Jason Kidd, each had the
opportunity to endear themselves to the fans.
But in an act of amazing greed, Robinson's agent
asked the Milwaukee Bucks to provide "Big Dog"
with a contract worth $100 million. If the Bucks
had complied, it would have been the richest
contract any athlete had ever signed, and pos-
sibly was worth more than the entire franchise.
And Jason Kidd had raised questions about his
character when he was involved in a hit-and-
run accident.

Piston's coach Don Chaney said, "The fans are
getting hungry—*hungry*—and are getting tired of
immature athletes. They want something better."

So the fans can be forgiven for taking immediately to the third person chosen in the draft,
Grant Hill. Hill had starred in some of the most
exciting college playoff games. He somehow managed to display excellent basketball skills while
at the same time being a "nice guy." It helps that
he had a different background from most other
sports athletes. Larry Bird, Anfernee Hardaway,
and many others were born in poverty; their
only way out was through basketball. Grant
Hill's parents, on the other hand, were successful and well educated. Calvin Hill was a Pro
Bowl football player with the Dallas Cowboys.
Janet Hill is a respected member of Washington D.C.'s power elite. Grant Hill grew up in a
pleasant suburb; he never learned the "play-
ground" brand of basketball, which involves
trash-talking and trying to squash your opponents into the dirt.

A day after playing in the 1995 All-Star Game, Grant Hill accepted his Men's College Basketball Performer of the Year Award at the ESPY Awards ceremony.

Even today Grant does not insult or bait his opponents on the court. He learned good manners from his father, who never spiked the ball or did a dance after scoring a touchdown. When Grant talks on court, he says things like "Nice move."

Just because he doesn't taunt other players does not mean he is afraid of them. "I know I'm just as confident as other guys," Hill says. "But when I make a basket, I don't pump my fist. I turn it into positive energy on the defensive end. That's the way I've always been, even to the point where I was criticized for not showing more emotion on the court."

Hill did not become conceited by being the top vote getter in the All-Star Game. He was just happy to be at the game itself. At the arena in Phoenix, Arizona, he looked around at the other players warming up and told reporters, "It's like I won a fantasy contest and get to hang out with the All Stars." He agreed with fellow first-time All Star Vin Baker of the Milwaukee Bucks that he "felt like getting everyone's autograph." When asked how he thought he would do in the game, Hill responded, "I don't plan on scoring a zillion points. I'm just trying to get over being in awe."

When the All-Star Game started, Hill did not play as if he was in awe at all. Early in the game Anfernee Hardaway of the Orlando Magic sent a high pass towards the basket. Grant Hill leaped, caught the ball in both hands, and dunked mightily as he descended. The alley-oop play gave the East team its second field goal and showed how basketball could be fun, flashy, and exciting at the same time.

Hill finished the game with 10 points on 5 of 8 shooting from the field. He handed out 3 assists and had 2 steals in 20 minutes of playing time. He was also 0 for 4 on free-throw attempts, showing the one gap in his game—Hill has never been more than an average shooter at the line. The West won the game 139-112.

As further proof of his popularity, after the All-Star Game, Grant made an appearance on "Late Night with David Letterman." He showed off his piano-playing skills by jamming with Paul Schafer and the band.

Grant next made an appearance on ESPN to pick up an ESPY award for being Men's College Basketball Performer of the Year. On the following Tuesday, he woke up at 4:30 a.m. to get on a plane back to Detroit and join his teammates for a morning practice. That evening he scored 25 points—sinking 11 in a row—as the Pistons defeated a strong New York Knicks team, 106-94.

Being popular had long been important to Hill. "I guess I always wanted to be liked by everybody," Grant said. "Here my father was in sports, my parents had money, and I'm thinking that if I do well in sports, people will get jealous of me and not like me. I didn't want to seem better than everybody else. Eventually, I realized I *was* better."

And soon he recognized that being better helped make him popular. Now Hill is willing to admit, "I want to beat you and embarrass you bad. But I don't want people to know that. It's like a little secret I keep to myself."

2

BORN TO GREATNESS

Grant Hill's parents, Calvin and Janet, were not born rich. Calvin's father, Henry Hill, was born in South Carolina and worked as a farmer. After moving to Baltimore during the Great Depression of the 1930s, he got a job as a construction worker.

Calvin excelled in school and on the football field. He chose to go to Yale University, in New Haven, Connecticut, one of the premier places for academic studies. Yale offered no athletic scholarships, yet was thrilled to have Hill decide to attend there instead of the other schools that also wanted him. Hill was probably the most popular person on campus, starring on the football field and majoring in history.

A fellow Yalie at that time was Garry Trudeau. He was already drawing a cartoon strip that later became known as "Doonesbury." Trudeau based a recurring character in Doonesbury on Calvin Hill. In the cartoon, "Calvin" was a

Calvin Hill, Grant's father, was a standout football player at Yale University.

straight-talking, civil-rights-protesting student—and the only black in the football huddle.

The Dallas Cowboys, a new franchise in the National Football League, made Calvin Hill their number one draft in 1969, which stunned a lot of people. Graduates of Ivy League schools do not usually go on to play in the pros at all, let alone be a top draft pick. Few fans had ever heard of Hill.

In his first game as a Cowboy, Hill threw a halfback option pass for a touchdown. In his second game, he ran for 138 yards, breaking the Cowboy's single-game rushing record. "By the time our season ended," a proud Cowboy's coach Tom Landry pointed out, "our unknown rookie, who some observers had thought was a wasted draft pick, had done nothing less than tie Jim Brown's all-time rookie rushing totals and play a leading role in an 11-2-1 Cowboys' season." Hill was named Rookie of the Year.

Calvin Hill (left) was a true student of the game. Here he goes over the playbook with teammate "Bullet" Bob Hayes.

While on the Cowboys, Calvin studied theology at Southern Methodist University. He had a reputation on the team of being a straight arrow, someone who rarely used foul language. He was a true student of the game. When Coach Landry introduced a new play in the lockerroom, Calvin could be expected to ask Landry to break it down and explain it further. "He had to know exactly what everybody was doing on each play—which actually made him a better football player," recalled teammate "Bullet" Bob Hayes.

Calvin was not the only intellectual on the team. There was also offensive lineman John Wilbur, a graduate of Stanford University; quarterback Craig Morton, who went to Berkeley; and tight end Jean Fugett, a graduate of Amherst College. Quarterback Roger Staubach was also a thinking man's player, a true straight arrow, as was Hill.

While other players were concerned about how good they looked, Hill could not be bothered by his attire. One year, Calvin had his arm in a sling and could not play in the NFC final against the Minnesota Vikings. He stood on the sidelines wearing an "old gray sweater, old brown slacks, and some old yellow tennis shoes," a teammate remembered. Janet asked the teammate to tell Calvin to change into something more presentable, but Calvin just did not care.

In 1971, the Cowboys had put together a great team. Their "Doomsday Defense" featured Jethro Pugh, Bob Lilly, Lee Roy Jordan, Mel Renfro, and later Harvey Martin, and Ed "Too-Tall" Jones. On offense, the Cowboys had Mike Ditka at tight end, one of the fiercest competitors ever to play the game. Lance Rentzel and Bob Hayes, "the world's fastest human," were outstanding wide receivers, as was Drew Pearson, who joined the team in 1973. Rayfield Wright and Ralph Neely anchored a solid offensive line.

The Cowboys had two fine quarterbacks in Roger Staubach and Craig Morton. Landry had a quandary over whom to start; in one game against the Chicago Bears, he had them alternate every other offensive play. The strategy worked—the Cowboys gained 480 yards that game—but eventually Landry had to pick a starter, and he chose Staubach. Once he did, the Cowboys did not lose another game all season. They finished the year with 11 wins and 3 losses.

Staubach became the heart of the Cowboy team. Although he had an excellent college career, he was picked in only the tenth round of the 1964 draft. The reason for his not being picked sooner is because as a graduate of the U.S. Naval Academy, he could not join any team as a full-time player until he served five years in the Navy. Dallas knew he was worth the wait. In his career with the Cowboys, Staubach led them to three Super Bowls and numerous last-second victories.

In the 1971 playoffs, the Cowboys knocked off the Minnesota Vikings 20-9 and the San Francisco 49ers, 14-3. They then played the Miami Dolphins in the Super Bowl and crushed them 24-3. Calvin Hill, along with fellow backs Duane Thomas and Walt Garrison, gained a record 250 yards on the ground—more than the 185 yards Miami had rushing and passing combined. After the Cowboys won this game, they were known as "America's Team," the most popular team in all of American sports.

In 1972, Hill had a year to remember. It started off with the Cowboys winning the Super Bowl. Later that year, Hill became the first Cowboy to rush for over 1,000 yards in a season. In October of that year, his wife gave birth to a healthy child.

Janet Hill was also a woman of achievement. She attended the elite Wellesley College, where one of her friends and roommates was Hillary Rodham. Hillary later became a lawyer, married

Bill Clinton, and became First Lady of the United States.

Janet Hill trained to be a mathematician. After graduation, she moved to Washington, D.C., where she got a job with a consulting company. She eventually became partners with Clifford Alexander, a former secretary of the Army. Janet's nickname was "the General" because she ran a tight household. Still, once Grant was older, she made time to call him every day at four o'clock, even stepping out of important meetings to do so.

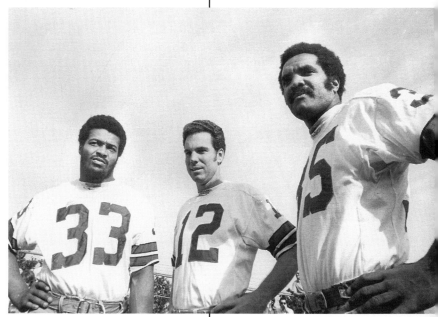

Duane Thomas, Roger Staubach, and Calvin Hill formed the nucleus of the Cowboy's offense. A few days after this photo was taken, they helped Dallas pound the Miami Dolphins into submission in the Super Bowl.

Grant Hill was born on October 5, 1972. That week, his father was named *Associated Press* Offensive Player of the Week. He had an outstanding game against Pittsburgh. He threw a 55-yard option pass for a touchdown as the Cowboys nipped the Steelers, 17-13.

Calvin had been hoping for a son but expecting a girl—so much so, he had only come up with a list of girl's names. For three days, the infant had no name. Then Roger Staubach came to visit in the hospital. Calvin and Janet read off a list of boy's names they had hastily prepared, and Staubach picked the one he liked the most. "It's time to name him, and we're going to name him Grant."

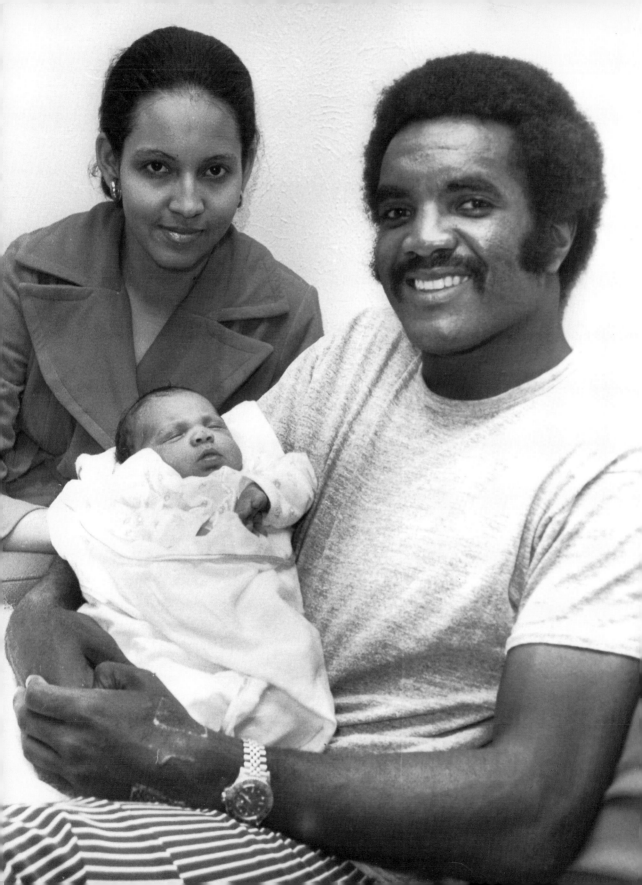

3

BORN INTO A ROYAL FAMILY

Grant's friends called his family "the Huxtables," the name of the family in the top-rated sitcom of the time, "The Cosby Show." In that show, Bill Cosby played a successful doctor, and Phylicia Rashad played his wife, a successful lawyer. They lived in a posh Brooklyn brownstone together with a lovable brood of kids. Some critics attacked the show as unrealistic, but Bill Cosby was onto something in depicting the life and times of an upper middle class black family. Blacks on television too often had been ghetto dwellers ("Good Times"), junk dealers ("Sanford & Son"), or servants ("Maude"). "The Jeffersons" was the only previous sitcom to show a successful black businessman, and much of its humor was derived from the seeming oddity of a nouveau riche black couple living in a fancy apartment and having a maid. "The Cosby Show" let the world know that there was a black upper

Grant Hill was an immediate celebrity. "The Littlest Cowboy," as the press called him, posed with his proud parents just hours after being born.

class and that their lives were genuinely worth watching.

Grant Hill is the first to admit he had a privileged childhood. "I know this sounds funny," he said. "but it was almost like being born into a royal family and being raised like a prince, being taught one day to become a king. Not just how to be an athlete, but how to do things right."

Calvin and Janet Hill have said that they did not raise Grant to be either an athlete or a king. They just wanted him to be a "man of character." They provided a loving household for him in Reston, Virginia, a beautiful, upper class suburb of Washington, D.C. Their house was filled with expensive works of art; their lawn was a great place for a kid to play ball. Calvin lived there even as he finished out his career playing for the Cleveland Browns. (After leaving the Dallas Cowboys, he also played with the Washington Redskins and the Hawaiians of the World Football League for one year.) Later, he got a job closer to home—as vice president of a baseball team, the Baltimore Orioles.

Famous people often visited the Hills' abode. Many were athletes, such as Roger Staubach, Miami Dolphin wide receiver Paul Warfield, and Cleveland Browns tight end Ozzie Newsome, but all were also smart people with other interests in life. "I think that just listening to my friends talk, Grant picked up a lot of things—the dos and don'ts of being in public," Calvin said. "There was a sense that you have to do something with fame and fortune—that there was a certain power in being an athlete."

The Hills were strict parents. They would not allow Grant to use the telephone except for one hour a week—and on Saturday only. Once, when

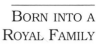

As a high school student, Grant Hill could do it all: dribble, pass, rebound, play defense—and, of course, shoot the ball.

Grant broke curfew, Janet took his watch and threw it against a wall. "You don't use it, anyway," she exclaimed. (Later she had the watch fixed and presented it to him on his birthday, gift-wrapped.)

"My parents stressed the importance of education," Grant said. "Everything I needed, everything I had to hear, was right at home."

Both Calvin and Janet were only children, which meant Grant had no aunts, uncles, or cousins.

Hill was invited to numerous all-star games before he became a pro.

He, too, was an only child, and so he got the full amount of his parents' love and attention.

At the age of six, his parents took him to London, England. Calvin Hill was friendly with Kingman Brewster, who had been the president of Yale during Calvin's years there; Brewster was then the U.S. Ambassador to England. Calvin and Janet brought Grant along as they visited Brewster in his office in the American Embassy; while they talked, Grant practiced doing headstands and cartwheels. On a later vacation, the three Hills went to Egypt.

At the age of 12, Calvin and Janet took Grant to the Yale-Harvard football game. Grant got confused when famous writer Norman Mailer and the president of Harvard University, Derek Bok, were pointed out to him. The president of Yale, A. Bartlett Giamatti, came to Grant's assistance and cleared up who was who.

Grant's first sport was soccer. He loved the game and credits it with teaching him agility and the importance of having a quick first step. Music was as important to him as sports. "I didn't have a Little League father pressuring me to play football or basketball," Grant said. "I played instruments, like piano, the bass, trombone."

His parents did not want him to take up football and told him that he could not even think of playing it until he reached the ninth grade. They wanted to protect him from being hurt while still young and growing, or having people compare him to his father before he was ready. As it turned out, Grant had discovered another sport by that time and never played a single down in high school or college football.

When Grant entered ninth grade, Coach Wendell Byrd of South Lakes High School asked Calvin to try out for the varsity basketball team. Grant did not want to play for the varsity. The year before, he served as water boy for the ninth-grade team. He had a lot of friends on that team and was looking forward to playing with them on the junior varsity team. So he said no to the coach. Then, as Hill recalled, "Coach Byrd told me to go home and talk to my dad."

Grant went home and talked to his father. He was horrified to discover that Coach Byrd had already talked with Calvin. And Calvin had already decided Grant should play with the varsity if he could make the team. "I started crying," Hill later recalled. "I accused him of child abuse. I said, 'You can't make me do something that I don't want to do.' He just said, 'You're gonna play.'"

Of course, Grant made the varsity team.

Although Grant loved football as a child when his father was still playing professionally, he changed his mind about the game at an early age. One day, Calvin came to pick Grant up after school, and they watched the high school team practicing in the late summer heat for a few minutes. Calvin suggested that next year Grant would be out there with them. "I looked," recalled Grant, "and said, 'I am not going to be out in this hot weather. I'm going to be in that air-conditioned gym.'"

The most important thing to Grant at this age was that he be liked. He was embarrassed by his family's money and success. One day, Calvin came in his Porsche to pick Grant up from school. Grant went red and asked his father to use the family Volkswagen in the future. "I just didn't want to appear better than others," Grant said.

Once, the principal of South Lakes High school invited Calvin to speak in front of the student body. Calvin accepted, but Grant did not hear his father's presentation. He pretended to be sick and hid in the nurse's office.

At the age of 13, Grant's basketball skills were already outstanding. One day, his father thought Grant was feeling a little too cocky about himself and challenged him to a game of one-on-one.

Calvin was 38 at the time and still quite fit. He used to boast, "Grant, you're good. But you've only got half my genes. Imagine if you had the other half." But Grant's genes were just fine. He was already 6′3″, one inch shorter than his dad. Father and son stepped out onto the driveway. Calvin went at Grant for all he was worth, but Grant won easily.

Calvin could not believe it. He demanded a rematch. Grant won again.

"I didn't want Grant to feel he had to be an athlete," Calvin said later. "But the fact that he has turned out to be one pleases me. It's like General Douglas MacArthur," he continued, referring to the World War II hero. "His father was a general too, and the son totally eclipsed him."

"It was no big deal," Grant jokes. "I thought of him as just another chump out there on the basketball court."

The person who gave Grant the most competition in one-on-one games was his best friend, Mike Ellison. Ellison challenged Hill to play long hours of full-court one-on-one games. This helped Grant greatly to improve his ball-handling skills.

In his junior and senior years, Hill led his high school team to state championships. He was name a high school all-American. College recruiters came to see him play and badgered him with requests to attend their schools.

Some recruiters suggested their college could provide Grant with improper bonuses—use of a free car, a no-show job, or just someone to do his laundry. Grant immediately dismissed any possibility of attending those universities. "What motivates Grant is to show that his success has nothing to do with what he is given," Calvin said, "and everything to do with what he earns."

From 1984 to 1988, Calvin rewarded Grant for his good grades and burgeoning basketball skills by taking him to the semifinals and finals of the NCAA championship. The two had a great time each year, staying up late, messing up their hotel room, and watching great basketball. They did not know it at the time, but they were preparing for Grant's own participation in some of the greatest games in NCAA finals history.

When it came time for Grant Hill to decide where to go to college, one place stood out. Duke University offered a top-notch academic program, one of the best basketball programs in the country, and the college is situated in Durham, North Carolina, a not-too-long drive from Hill's home in Virginia.

Founded in 1838, the school renamed itself in 1924 after James Buchanan Duke, who left the school an enormous endowment in his will. Duke had become one of the wealthiest men in the world selling cigarettes and other tobacco products. The large campus features beautiful green lawns, a terrific library, world-renowned professors, and an enthusiastic student body. Sometimes 5,000 people would show up just to watch the Duke basketball team practice—an amazing number given that the entire student enrollment was only 11,000.

Freshman Grant Hill zips a pass as Alonzo Jamison of the University of Kansas tries to defend in the 1991 NCAA championship game.

While other Duke teams alternate between good years and bad, the basketball teams were almost always competitive. Duke had enjoyed some of its best seasons just before Grant Hill showed up. Indeed, bestselling author John Feinstein had just written a book about the Blue Devils, whom he dubbed "Forever's Team."

For many years in a row, Duke had at least one or two upperclassmen who got a lot of the glory on the ball court. Mike Gminski, Mark Alarie, Johnny Dawkins, and Danny Ferry all had the experience to help lead their club, and Coach Mike Krzyzewski was happy to showcase their talent as they played out their eligibility and looked to turn pro the following year. In addition, these seniors helped groom the younger players, knowing that soon they would have their chance to shine.

In 1988, the team had recently lost Johnny Dawkins and Mark Alarie, but Danny Ferry and Phil Henderson led Duke to the Final Four of the NCAA tournament, where they lost to the University of Kansas. The next year, Christian Laettner joined the team. Again the Blue Devils went to the Final Four, this time losing to upstart Seton Hall University.

After the 1989 season, Ferry graduated. (He was a high pick in the NBA draft, but held out a year from joining the team that chose him, the Cleveland Cavaliers; instead, he played ball in Italy and studied at Oxford University in England). But Duke added the skillful guard Bobby Hurley to the team. This time, Duke made it to the NCAA champion game. They were pitted against a marvelous University of Nevada, Las Vegas team. Duke played them tight for the first half, but UNLV went on an 18-0 run early in the second half and ended up crushing Duke by a margin of 30 points.

After the 1989-1990 season, Phil Henderson and Alaa Abdelnaby departed. Duke fans were counting on Christian Laettner to pick up the mantle of leadership. But they were also hoping some new star would emerge so that the basketball team could continue to compete at the highest level in years ahead. Would that star be the very young-looking and gangling Grant Hill?

Mike Krzyzewski (pronounced kerSHEVski) was one of the most famous coaches in college basketball. He had led Army's basketball team to some of their best years before joining Duke in 1981. The 1982 and 1983 Duke teams were the only ones he had coached to end the season with losing records. Each team since 1984 had won at least 20 games a season; each team since 1985 had lost fewer than 10 games a season. He was one of the first coaches to sign a deal with a major sneaker manufacturer which paid him and Duke University millions of dollars. His only disappointment—Duke had been to four championship games, and had lost them all.

Coach K, as he was widely called, knew that Duke's chance of getting to a third straight NCAA Final Four would be determined by how much Hill was willing to become a star himself, to "jump his place in line." Coach K wanted Hill to establish his presence on court immediately, and not just serve as a table setter for the older players.

Grant was taken aback by all the pressure and fan adulation he received as soon as he arrived at Duke. He did not even know if Coach K would allow him to start, and already people were looking to him to lead the team to the next level of excellence. "In high school, I knew everyone from

Hill (left), Brian Davis (number 23), and Christian Laettner (far right) celebrate after helping Duke win the 1991 college basketball championship.

growing up with them. I was just one of the fellows," he said. "It wasn't anything like, 'ooh, you're Grant Hill.' There were people asking for my autograph and they were expecting so much —it was like if you didn't do what they thought you should be doing, you were letting them down."

Hill started off the Duke season well. He scored in double figures during his first six games, the first Blue Devil to do that since Johnny Dawkins. But later in the season he broke his nose and had a painful hip pointer which kept him out of three games. His natural inclination was to be selfless on the court, more interested in feeding the ball to an open teammate than in trying to force a shot.

"A kid like Grant needs to be helped to get to his rightful position, to realize that he's really that good," Coach K said. "Grant being Grant, he wants to be asked to advance in the line. He'll always be very sensitive toward everyone else in line, even when he's at the head of it."

Duke's first big test came in January, 1990. In their first interconference game, Duke was trounced by the University of Virginia. Coach K was furious and motivated his team never to take any opponents lightly. The young team took to his words and Duke finished the season with a 32-7 record.

The Blue Devils had an easy time in their first games in the NCAA tournament, beating Northeast Louisiana, Iowa, Connecticut, and St. John's by an average of nearly 16 points per game. The semifinals—better known as the Final Four—pitted them against the University of Nevada, Las Vegas, the team that had trounced them by 30 points, the widest margin ever in a championship game, the previous year. The Running Rebels were coached by the colorful Jerry "the Shark" Tarkanian and with Larry Johnson, Stacey Augmon, Anderson Hunt, and Greg Anthony, they were the only team ever to have four players score over 1,500 points in their college career.

UNLV was a near unanimous choice to win the tournament. They had not lost all season and were ranked number one from the start. *Sports Illustrated* opined that the team was even better than it had been the year before, when it had won the championship by crushing Duke. The magazine compared the Running Rebels favorably to the best teams in college basketball history and went on record saying, "The most beguiling question is not *whether* UNLV can be beaten, but whether the Rebels could *ever* be beaten."

"It's ridiculous," said Pete Gillen, coach of Xavier University. "Nobody will come within 10 points of them."

"If somebody beats them, it's an accident," added Jim Boeheim, coach of Syracuse University. "I know we can't."

Some Duke players were afraid of the matchup. Bobby Hurley had suffered nightmares about sharks after losing to "Shark" Tarkanian's team the year before. *Sports Illustrated* did not make things easier on Hurley when it recalled the previous year's final as the "goriest" in history.

Coach K gave Grant Hill the assignment of stopping Stacey Augmon, a forward whose game was similar to Grant's. Both were high-flyers who loved to slash their way to the hoop for powerful dunks.

Hill, the only starting freshman on the Blue Devils team, had a great game. "His suffocating defense on Stacey Augmon is a performance pro scouts still talk about," a journalist in the *New York Times* wrote several years later. The rest of the Duke team also played tough and got their revenge on the Running Rebels. Bobby Hurley got Greg Anthony into foul trouble and Christian Laettner hit several clutch baskets in the waning minutes. Duke won, 79-77.

The Blue Devils next met another team they had a grudge against in the finals of the NCAA championship. Kansas University had beaten Duke in the 1988 NCAA semi-finals. But Kansas had its own agenda. The Jayhawks had been ranked number one or two for 13 consecutive weeks the previous year, only to be upset in the second round of "March Madness."

Coach Roy Williams did not have many stars on his team—Adonis Jordan, the point guard, was perhaps the best known—but he had a deep bench and a game plan that called for fresh players to harass their opponents constantly.

Williams's best-laid plans did not work. Duke had too much fire power for Kansas's shorter team. Hill announced his presence on court in the second minute of the game. Grant "set the tone for the game by climbing high above the rim to throw down an alley-oop pass from Bobby Hurley," wrote a journalist in the *Washington Post*. Hill played a pivotal role, scoring 10 points, pulling down 8 rebounds, passing for 3 assists, plus blocking 2 shots and stealing 2 balls from the Jayhawks. The Blue Devils established a strong lead in the first half, which ended with them up 42-34. They cruised from there, winning 72-65 before 47,000 screaming fans.

The young freshman had taken the Blue Devils that extra distance, helping them to win their first national championship. *Sports Illustrated* honored Hill by putting him on the cover, and later calling him "transcendentally talented."

Only two people were not excited about the big win and the new star America was discovering. "I feel ordinary," an exhausted Grant Hill said after the Kansas game. And Calvin Hill mentioned to the press that during that week, Grant had done some less memorable things: he locked his car keys inside his car, had his phone disconnected because he had forgotten to pay his bills, and pretended to lock his dorm room every time he left because he had lost the key a month before. Calvin may have been a little bitter, as Grant had also forgotten to pick him up at the airport that week, too.

But it had been an amazing year for Grant. Not only had he led his team to a national championship while still only 18 years old, but he had also won an American Athletic Union (AAU) championship in St. Louis, Missouri, won a Junior National championship in Uruguay, and was named to the freshman All-American team.

Was it possible that at age 18, Hill had already enjoyed his greatest moments of basketball?

5

BREATHLESS

As a sophomore, Grant Hill helped lead Duke to its greatest season ever. Duke featured a new face in Cherokee Parks, a seven-foot center who could shoot and run the floor. (Parks, a colorful character, owed his name to his hippie parents; his favorite pastime, he admitted, was surfing.) Duke was rated number one for 18 straight weeks in the 1991-92 season. Hill spent two weeks on the sidelines with a sprained ankle, but even so the team finished with a 35-2 record and rolled into the playoffs on a tear.

Calvin Hill showed up for most of Grant's games. The television cameras loved to show at least one shot of him per game—in part because he was a celebrity, in part because he was the team's biggest booster, wearing his Duke hat and singing the Duke fighting song. But Janet and Grant Hill have another theory why Calvin

With Deron Feldhaus guarding him and only two seconds left in the game, Christian Laettner went up for a possible winning shot against the University of Kentucky.

always made it on camera—he knew the camera angles in every arena and picked out a seat where a cameraman could easily find him.

Duke's opponents in the first games in the NCAA tournament were Campbell University, the University of Iowa and Seton Hall University. Duke won by an average margin of over 20 points. Then, on March 28, 1992, the Blue Devils found themselves in one of the most exciting games in college basketball history. In the quarterfinals, Duke was matched against a hot team from the University of Kentucky. Kentucky was in its first postseason after a two-year probation due to NCAA rules violations, and they wanted to prove to a national audience that they could still compete against the best.

The last four minutes of the game had a national television audience biting its nails. In the last 31.5 seconds of the game each of the five possessions ended with a score. Each score resulted in a lead change.

Duke had jumped out to a lead, and with 11:08 remaining in the second half, the Blue Devils had a 67-55 advantage and were threatening to put the game out of reach for the Wildcats. Kentucky coach Rick Pitino told his team to play a full-court man-to-man defense, especially trying to harry Bobby Hurley, Duke's play-making guard. The plan worked, as Kentucky shut down the Blue Devils on their next possessions, and scored eight straight points themselves, six of them on three-pointers by Kentucky's go-to player, Jamal Mashburn.

A few minutes later, Christian Laettner got off a shot as Aminu Timberlake came over to defend. The two collided and Timberlake fell to the floor.

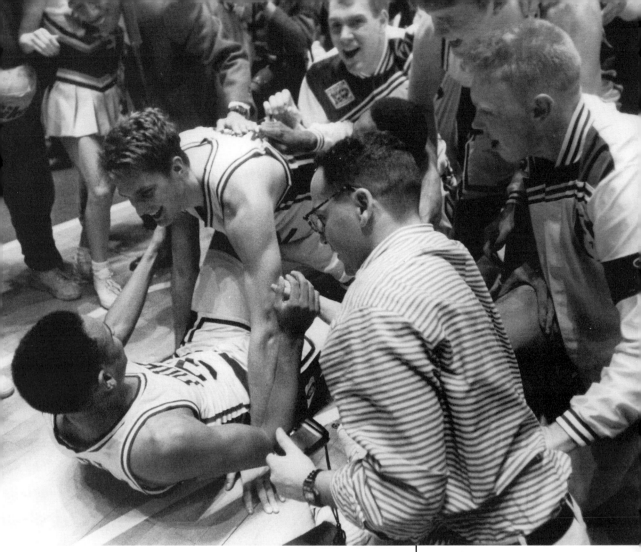

Laettner placed his right foot on Timberlake's mid-section as a kind of joke. Coach K was furious with Laettner, thinking the refs might eject the junior, or at least call a technical foul. But no whistle sounded. Laettner was having a phenomenal game. He would take 20 shots—10 from the free-throw line and 10 from the field—and make every one.

At the end of regulation, the score was tied at 93. Kentucky scored the first three points of overtime. Bobby Hurley spotted up for a three-point-

Pandemonium broke out in the stands and on the floor after the final shot of the Duke-Kentucky game. Christian Laettner and Grant Hill were knocked to the floor in the celebration.

er, missed it, but Grant Hill corralled the rebound. He jetted the ball back to Hurley, who took another three and this time nailed it.

The fireworks really started with 31 seconds left in the overtime period. Laettner hit a tough bank shot to put Duke up 100-99. Antonio Lang fouled Jamal Mashburn, who hit his two free throws. Mashburn then fouled Laettner; his free throws regained the lead for Duke, 102-101. With 7.8 seconds left, and the capacity crowd on its feet, Kentucky guard Sean Woods got the ball. He sliced through traffic and hit a running one-hander. Kentucky 103, Duke, 102. The Blue Devils called timeout with 2.1 seconds remaining on the clock.

In the stands, Janet Hill was consoling the father of Antonio Lang, when Calvin said, "Wait a minute." He was watching Coach K and thought he saw a glimmer of hope.

For his part, Coach K was telling his team, "We're going to win." He called for his hottest shooter, Christian Laettner, to try to get loose at the free-throw line. Now, how to get him the ball. "Grant, can you make the pass?" he asked.

"Yes, Coach," Hill said. "I can do it."

Earlier in the season, Duke had been in a similar situation. Grant had to throw a pass the length of the court, but with a defender in his face, the pass went wide and Wake Forest University won, one of two games Duke had lost all season. This time, Kentucky put no defender on Hill. He threw a 75-foot strike—as beautiful a pass as ever Roger Staubach had thrown to Calvin Hill in the closing seconds of a game—and Laettner caught it easily near the top of the key. He dribbled once, jumped, shot, and the ball fell threw the hoop as the time clock hit zero.

Watching the flight of his pass, Grant Hill thought of such movies as "The Natural" and *Hoosiers*, where slow-motion makes the climactic moments take an unusually long time. "Fate was on our side," he said later. "We were destined. Even if somebody had been (guarding) me, even if the pass had been off, Christian would have tipped it and it would have gone in. We still would have won somehow."

The crowd, which had been standing and cheering, was stunned. A moment of silence fell over much of the arena; some people started crying. One woman felt so dizzy she needed to be helped out of the stadium. Sean Woods, whose shot seemed to have won the game for the Wildcats, fell on the floor and did not move until a security officer came over and made sure he was still breathing.

"People who saw it knew it was a great game," said Coach Krzyzewski. "They didn't need any announcer or sportswriter to tell them it was. And not only Duke fans and Kentucky fans felt that way. Any basketball fan who saw it felt disbelief that any of it could happen."

Even President George Bush commented, "Did you see the end of that Duke game!"

"If you're asking for a way to describe what happened, you're asking the wrong person," Grant told a reporter. He said all he wanted to do was "Just relax, and watch the game over again, and celebrate for the next two days."

Two days later, Duke faced the University of Indiana in the semi-finals. The Hoosiers had won three championships under Coach Bobby Knight and never lost a Final Four game under his leadership.

The Hoosiers rolled up a 12-point halftime lead but Duke returned from the break playing per-

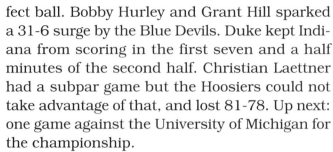

Hill defends against Chris Webber in the 1992 NCAA finals. Duke beat the University of Michigan to win its second straight championship.

fect ball. Bobby Hurley and Grant Hill sparked a 31-6 surge by the Blue Devils. Duke kept Indiana from scoring in the first seven and a half minutes of the second half. Christian Laettner had a subpar game but the Hoosiers could not take advantage of that, and lost 81-78. Up next: one game against the University of Michigan for the championship.

Michigan was an unusual team. They were led by the "Fab Five," a group of five freshmen, who had put together an amazing season. Chris Webber, Juwann Howard, and Jalen Rose were the most outstanding of the five. Rose and Hill were often compared because Rose's father had also been a famous athlete. The major difference was that Rose's father had abandoned his family and Jalen had not met his father until he was a famous athlete himself.

Again Duke got off to a slow start; Michigan ended the half with a one-point lead. But then Duke came out and blew them away in the second half. A 23-6 run gained control of the game for the Blue Devils, and they dominated the closing minutes, turning the score into a rout. Duke scored on 12 of its last 13 possessions and held the Wolverines to a mere 20 second-half points.

The Blue Devils won, 71-51. They were the only team in NCAA history to win by 20 points after being down at halftime. "Grant was the key to the game," said Coach K afterwards. Hill played 36 minutes, scored 18 points (second only to Christian Laettner), grabbed 10 rebounds (the most on the team), and passed for 5 assists (second to Bobby Hurley). He did this all while suffering from a bruised right knee that had people wondering whether he would even suit up for the game.

Duke was the first team to repeat as champions since the amazing John Wooden-coached UCLA teams of 1967-1973 and also the first number one ranked team to win the title since North Carolina State in 1982. During the tournament, Christian Laettner became the all-time NCAA tournament leading scorer and Bobby Hurley became its all-time leading assists man. Hurley was named the most valuable player of the 1992 tournament, but many people felt Grant Hill was more deserving, especially as he had shot much better, had fewer turnovers, grabbed far more rebounds, and passed for nearly as many assists.

Speaking of the 1991 and 1992 Final Fours, Coach K said, "Christian and Bobby were the MVPs, but the guy who played as well as anybody in those four games was Grant. But he didn't mind staying out of the limelight, because last year it was Christian's and Brian Davis's turn, and the year before that it was Christian's and even Greg Koubek's turn. Grant's made the biggest jump with his shot and his assertiveness and being consistently excellent. To make the next jump, he'll need to play without Bobby and be the leader."

6

PLAYING ALL
THE POSITIONS

After the 1991-92 season, Grant Hill was constantly in demand. He appeared on the Charlie Rose Show, an interview show for intellectuals on PBS. He made a speech at the National Association of Basketball Coaches' Issues Forum.

In 1993, Laettner joined the pro ranks, taken as the second player in the draft (after Shaquille O'Neal) by the Minnesota Timberwolves. Duke was not the same team. Grant was named the nation's best defensive player, but the Blue Devils were upset in the second round of the NCAA tournament by the University of California, 82-77. Cherokee Parks hurt his ankle just before halftime and did not return to the game. Still, Duke put up a good struggle, even going ahead 77-76 with under three minutes left to play. But after a missed shot, Cal's Jason Kidd emerged from the pack with the free ball; he threw in a

Hill goes past Jason Kidd for two points in the 1993 NCAA playoffs. But the University of California upset Duke, as the Blue Devils failed to make it to the championship game for the first time in four years.

45

wild shot while being fouled. Bobby Hurley, playing in his last collegiate game, missed a three pointer. Cal's Lamond Murray rebounded and hit two free throws to finish the scoring.

"Our kids fought valiantly," Coach K said. "We didn't lose the ball game. Cal won it."

The *New York Times* raved about the level of play, calling it the "best game the 1993 NCAA tournament has offered."

For 1993-1994, Duke had a new point guard in Jeff Capel and a new shooting guard in Chris Collins. But everyone knew the key to the success of their season was Grant Hill. "Grant can play every position," said Coach K. "And has. And will."

Hill played more in his senior year than any previous year—Coach K gave him an average of just over four minutes to catch his breath per game. Grant was indispensable to the team, taking more shots and free throws, scoring more points, pulling down more rebounds, and passing for more assists than he had ever done before. Only his shooting percentage went down, as the burden of being the lead scorer on the team meant he had to force some difficult shots.

Hill suddenly displayed an outside touch that had been little seen before. In his first two seasons with Duke, he took only 3 three-point shots, making only 1.

In his junior season, he had tried 14, making only 4. In the 1993-94 season, Hill started pouring in the threes, trying 100 and hitting on 39, for a fine success ratio of .390. Defenses now had to worry about him close to the basket and when he roamed the perimeter.

With Hill leading the way, Duke put together a terrific 26-5 season. The Blue Devils were

ranked number two in their sector for the NCAA tournament. They posted easy victories against Texas Southern, Michigan State, and Marquette University in their first three matchups, winning each game by at least 10 points. They then faced top-ranked Purdue University, which was led by Glenn "Big Dog" Robinson.

Robinson averaged over 30 points per game in leading the nation in scoring in 1994. Both he and Hill were 6'8" forwards and coming off terrific games. Hill had scored 16 of his 22 points in the second half in the Marquette game. Robinson had poured in 44 to help Purdue defeat

The big matchup in the 1994 NCAA playoffs pitted high-scoring Glenn Robinston against Grant Hill. Hill and the Blue Devils were able to keep "Big Dog" and the Purdue Boilermakers in check and move on in the playoffs.

Kansas. Purdue's coach, Gene Keady, knew Hill well from when he coached him on the 1991 Pan American Games team. "We've got to keep him out of the paint, because he'll destroy you when he gets in there," Keady acknowledged before the game.

Robinson and Hill had never played each other, although they met during a photo shoot of the All-American team arranged by *Playboy* magazine the previous summer. "The only difference between our games is that I shoot more than he does and he gets more assists than I do," Robinson said. "But if they need him to score 40 points, believe me he can. If I have to get six or seven assists, I'd do my best."

Purdue was ranked number one in the sec-

Early in the championship game against the University of Arkansas, Grant Hill took a painful fall. Hill returned and had a fine second half, but the Razorbacks won the tight game and the championship in 1994.

tor, having won 29 of their 32 games thus far in the season. Duke managed to keep a lead for most of the game, as the battle between Hill and Robinson never really emerged. Cherokee Parks, Antonio Lang, and Hill shut down Big Dog. When Hill had to leave the game with 10 minutes left after having picked up his fourth foul, the crowd in Knoxville, Tennessee, expected Robinson to come to life. "I said a little prayer," said Lang. Robinson immediately hit a jumper to shave Duke's lead down to 46-43. But then Lang and Parks hit two baskets each, and Jeff Capel, a freshman guard for Duke, continued his torrid shooting—he scored all of his 19 points in the second half. Robinson managed only 13 points on just 6 of 22 shooting, his worst game of the season. Duke won, 69-60.

The Blue Devils' next opponent was a Cinderella team from Florida. The Gators were making their first trip to the Final Four after playing in their first NCAA tournament only seven years before. The Gators powered their way to a 39-32 halftime lead, only the third lead Duke had allowed an opponent all tournament long. It was also the largest lead Duke had allowed, and soon it ballooned to 13 points. But Hill showed his shooting touch, scoring 25 points in the game— including a 13-foot jumper that gave them a lead at 61-60—and Duke then pulled away for a 70-65 victory. The win returned Duke to the championship game for the third time in the four years Hill had played with the team and the fourth time in the past five years for the Blue Devils. Their opponent: the number-one-ranked University of Arkansas Razorbacks.

President Bill Clinton attended the game, admitting he was a fan of Arkansas; he had served as governor of the state for 12 years. The Razorbacks boasted that a game against them was "40 minutes of hell," as few teams could hope to stop both the inside power of forward Corliss Williamson and the outside shooting touch of Corey Beck and Scotty Thurman.

Early in the game, Grant took a tumble and hurt his lower back. He recovered quickly and ended up pulling down a team-high 14 rebounds. Still, Arkansas focused much of their defensive pressure on Grant and largely kept the ball out of his hands.

Duke played hard, though they clearly were the more tired team. Three minutes into the second half, they pushed to a 48-38 lead, with Hill's play sparking them emotionally. But the Razorbacks immediately started coming back; fans could sense the momentum swinging their way. Arkansas tied the game and started to extend to a lead when Grant Hill hit a clutch three pointer to tie the score at 70 with one minute, fifteen seconds left in the game. Arkansas took a timeout.

When play resumed, the Razorbacks tried to get the ball to Corliss Williamson, but he was triple teamed. They looked for Scottie Thurman, but he was covered as well. Dwight Stewart, a burly, baby-faced forward, was open. He fumbled the pass but he picked it up, and with 51 seconds left, hit a long three-pointer with Antonio Lang in his face. "That's the first time that anybody has ever made a shot like that on me. I mean, ever," Lang said later.

"That's a shot we wanted him to take," Jeff Capel said. "And then that wound up the shot that knocked us out. We couldn't recover from that. There was plenty of time, 51 seconds, but I think our younger guys, including myself, panicked a little bit after that shot."

For the remaining plays, Duke put up three shots, all misses (although Cherokee Parks did score off a rebound), and then fouled the Razorbacks hoping they would miss their free throws. They did not. Chris Collins misfired on two bombs for Duke, and the game was over. The Blue Devils had limited the Razorbacks to hitting only 39% of their shots—by far their worst outing of the tournament—but it was not enough.

"I thought this was one of the best games we've ever had in the NCAA tournament and I've been in about 50 of them," said Coach K after the game. Actually he had only been in 48, but his teams had won 39 of those games.

Duke had lost its fifth NCAA championship game—a record—but they had also clearly become a dynasty—the longest-running dominant basketball team in America.

Grant Hill ended his NCAA tournament play with a superb record of 18 wins and 2 losses. He now had new horizons to explore.

7

MOTOR CITY BLUES

For most years of their existence, the Detroit Pistons were not a great team. Center Bob Lanier was their best player for over 10 years; Lanier is a member of the Basketball Hall of Fame, but he never got to play for an NBA championship.

In the early 1980s, the front office of the Pistons started doing things right. They had six good drafts in a row, picking Isiah Thomas and Kelly Tripucka in 1981, Cliff Levingstone and Ricky Pierce in 1982, Antoine Carr, Tony Campbell, Joe Dumars, and John Sally in the next four years.

The front office also made some good trades and put together a dynamic team. Bill Laimbeer was the starting center, a tall banger with a good outside-shooting touch. Forward Dennis Rodman was a defensive dervish and John Sally could back up Laimbeer at center or switch over to power forward. Joe Dumars was a prototype

Hill immediately made his mark in the NBA. Opponents often felt the need to foul him to keep him from getting to the basket.

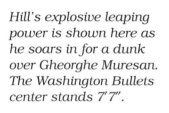

Hill's explosive leaping power is shown here as he soars in for a dunk over Gheorghe Muresan. The Washington Bullets center stands 7'7".

player at shooting guard, and guard Vinny Johnson provided firepower coming off the bench. Johnson was nicknamed "The Microwave" because he got hot so quickly.

Chuck Daly was recognized as a brilliant coach, but the heart of the team was Isiah Thomas, a six-foot-tall point guard who could do it all. He could dribble as well as anyone in the league, make dazzling passes that left the defensive team stunned, and when opponents tried to double team him, he could slice through amazingly small spaces and take the ball to the hoop. He was the recognized "go-to" guy on the Pistons, the player who wanted—and got—the ball in the closing seconds, when the game was going to be won or lost in the final possession.

The Pistons became known as the "Bad Boys." When Michael Jordan, Scottie Pippin, and the rest of the Chicago Bulls came to Detroit, they could count on being fouled hard if ever they got close to an easy basket. Patrick Ewing and the New York Knicks also counted their bruises in tough playoff matches against the Pistons. The physical play of Laimbeer, Rodman, and company might not have made them many friends around the NBA, but it was immensely successful. The Pistons won back-to-back championships, in 1988-89 and 1989-90.

But after the 1993 season, things started to go downhill fast for the Motor City team. Due to trades, they had no draft picks in 1987, 1988, and 1991. They picked low in the 1989 and 1990 drafts. Their selections—Kenny Battle and Lance Blanks—were not the sort of players who could help keep a great team on top.

In 1993, Detroit drafted Lindsey Hunter and Allan Houston, promising players, but the team decline only grew worse. Dennis Rodman was traded. Bill Laimbeer retired 11 games into the season and Isiah Thomas retired at the end of the year. In the 1993-94 season, the Pistons lost 62 out of the 82 games they played. Only the Dallas Mavericks had a worse record.

Sometimes a team's tribulations turn into its good luck. By performing so poorly, Detroit was rewarded with the third pick in the 1994 draft.

The Milwaukee Bucks had the first pick, and they took Glenn Robinson. The Dallas Mavericks used their second pick to select Jason Kidd. The Pistons were ecstatic to have the 6'8", 225-pound Grant Hill still available for their third pick. They did not hesitate.

Hill asked Lon Babby to be his agent. Instead of giving him a percentage as most agents get, Hill paid Babby by the hour for negotiating his contract with the Pistons. Babby did all right for Hill—securing a deal worth $45 million over eight years.

Hill also quickly signed a number of deals to endorse products. Schick asked him to be their spokesperson at the Schick NBA rookie game. Wilson featured him in a "stay in school" promotional advertisement and had him endorse their basketballs. Hill signed a two-year deal to promote the Ohio Art Company. Coca Cola inked him to a multi-year deal to act as Sprite's "global spokesman." Hill signed a three-year exclusive deal with trading card company Skybox International. In a particularly savvy move, Hill teamed up with GMC truck (which he drives), a very popular thing for a player from Detroit, where GM has its headquarters. Isiah Thomas had displeased local fans when he agreed to promote Toyota, a Japanese car manufacturer.

In perhaps his richest contract, agent Tom George of Advantage International Marketing put Grant together with Fila shoe. The sneaker Grant endorsed set all sorts of records when it came out. Over 14,000 pairs were sold in its first four days at Foot Locker. Michael Jordan, the previous record holder, sold 17,000 pairs of sneakers in his best week.

All told, these contracts pay Hill about $5 million a year. This nearly doubles what he makes for playing basketball.

Grant Hill was thrilled to be a Piston. "To be in the NBA, to be at the place that you've dreamed of all your life—it's like you can't believe that you're finally there," Hill said. I'm still like a little kid in this game, playing against guys that I grew up idolizing, like Scottie Pippen and Charles Barkley and Dominique Wilkins. It's wild even being on the same court as them. And then when you do something nice, like a move on them or whatever, it makes you feel good."

Other basketball aficionados were feeling good about Hill, too. In Hill's first game as a pro, the Detroit Pistons took on the Los Angeles Lakers. Del Harris, coach of the Lakers, told the media that he thought Grant Hill was a future Hall of Famer. He said this minutes *before* the game started.

Hill averaged over 20 points in his first six games although it became clear that the Pistons still did not have enough manpower to challenge the best teams. Hill's average started to dip as opponents realized that he and Joe Dumars were Detroit's only real offensive threats. If they could shut down one or both of them, no other Piston would be able to carry the team to victory.

Hill hated losing, but he loved getting to meet and play against other NBA stars. When the Pistons were in Philadelphia to play the 76ers, Julius Erving, one of his childhood idols, came to the game. Erving gave Grant some advice, and then gave him his phone number. Hill went to the team bus, pulled out his cellular phone, and called the number four or five times, just to listen to Dr. J's answering machine.

The fans were enthralled with Hill, too. Even supporters of other teams showed up early at basketball arenas, hoping to catch sight of the young rookie. Many called out to him, hoping he'd look their way just for a moment. On March 16, the Pistons were in Cleveland to play the Cavaliers. Hill went to his locker to find that someone had stolen his uniform and warmup suit. Luckily, Pistons trainer Tony Harris had a backup so Grant did not have to miss the game.

Grant signs many autographs wherever he goes. Yet he is something of a loner. He does not go out of his way to pal around with his teammates, often choosing to eat alone, go to bookstores alone, drive alone, go to movies alone. He does not frequent bars; in fact, Grant does not drink because he knows of people whose lives have been ruined by alcohol.

Becoming a pro basketball player requires a player to make many tough adjustments. There's the longer schedule, the increased travel, the tougher competition. One of the toughest adjustments for Grant has been dealing with the press. Even though reporters have treated Hill well, he has to be very careful with what he says—and listens to.

At the end of 1994-95 season, Jason Kidd and Grant Hill were named co-winners of the NBA Rookie of the Year Award.

When journalists rushed to compare Hill to Michael Jordan, Grant responded by saying, "I just try to ignore it. It's something I don't really like.... I try not to listen to any critiques, be they positive or negative."

"Grant does have similar moves (to Jordan)," said teammate Joe Dumars. "But I've been very cautious not to throw that label on him."

It was hard for Hill not to listen, considering how much he was being talked about. "You see how comfortable he plays with veteran Joe Dumars when they connect for spectacular plays," said Bob Zuffelato, a scout for the Toronto Raptors. "He's a rookie yet mature beyond his years. That tells you a lot about Grant Hill."

Hill formed a great partnership with the senior Piston guard. "I'm in a great spot. Joe Dumars is one of the smartest, probably the smartest player in the NBA," Grant said. "And I consider myself a student of the game. You can't ask for a better learning situation than that."

In his first season, Hill averaged just under 20 points per game. He showed his all-around talent by also pulling down 445 rebounds (including 125 off the offensive boards), handing out 353 assists, making 124 steals, and only turning the ball over 202 times in 70 games.

The Pistons finished the 1994-95 season with a losing record. But they had a major source of pride: Hill shared Rookie of the Year honors with Jason Kidd. Each received 43 votes out of a possible 105. Glenn Robinson was third with 15 votes. (The only other tie for this award came in 1971 when Dave Cowens of the Boston Celtics tied with Geoff Petrie of the Portland Trailblazers.) Hill was also named to the NBA All-Rookie first team.

In his second NBA season, Hill improved his scoring average to 20.2 points per game, and his rebounding also improved significantly. He also was the leading All-Star vote-getter for the second straight year, as the fans recognized his hard work.

And although Detroit didn't make it out of the first round of the NBA playoffs, Hill was a member of a championship team—the U.S. Men's Basketball Team, which won the gold medal at the 1996 Summer Olympics in Atlanta. Grant played in six games and averaged 9.7 points per game.

In 1997, Grant elevated his game, helping Detroit win 54 games. He increased his scoring average to 21.4 points per game, pulled down nine rebounds per game, and dished out 7.3 assists each contest. He was named to the All-Star team for the third time, and many NBA fans acknowledge him as the best young basketball player in a league full of young stars.

Although Grant is in his mid-twenties, he is already thinking about how he would like to be remembered after his playing days are done. He would like kids to dream about him, the way he used to dream about his idols, Julius Erving and tennis player Arthur Ashe.

Once, in college, Hill invited a friend from the University of North Carolina team to stay at his parent's house. Brian Reese looked at the Hills' lavish estate and asked Grant, "Why do you play basketball? The reason I play is to get my mother out of this particular project. You got it made. Why are you out there playing?"

"I play because I love the game," Hill responded.

Fans see how Grant plays the game for love, and they love watching the way he plays.

STATISTICS

GRANT HENRY HILL

Year	Team	G	FGM	FGA	Pct	FTM	FTA	Pct	REB	AST	PTS	AVG
1990-91	Duke	36	160	310	.516	81	133	.609	185	79	402	11.2
1991-92	Duke	33	182	298	.611	99	246	.733	167	134	483	14.0
1992-93	Duke	26	185	320	.578	94	126	.746	166	72	468	18.0
1993-94	Duke	34	218	472	.462	116	185	.703	233	176	591	17.4
TOTALS		129	745	1400	.532	390	559	.698	771	461	1924	14.9

Year	Team	G	FGM	FGA	Pct	FTM	FTA	Pct	REB	AST	PTS	AVG
1994-95	Det	70	508	1064	.477	374	511	.732	445	353	1394	19.9
1995-96	Det	80	564	1221	.462	485	646	.751	783	548	1618	20.2
1996-97	Det	80	625	1259	.496	450	633	.711	720	584	1710	21.4
TOTALS		230	1697	3544	.479	1309	1790	.731	1948	1485	4722	20.5

G	game
FGA	field goals attempted
FGM	field goals made
PCT	percent
FTA	free throws attempted
FTM	free throws made
REB	rebounds
AST	assists
PTS	points
AVG	scoring average

GRANT HILL
A CHRONOLOGY

1972   Calvin Hill wins a Super Bowl ring with the Dallas Cowboys; Grant Hill is born on October 5 and given his name by Roger Staubach

1991   Hill helps Duke wreak revenge on UNLV and Kansas en route to the Blue Devils' first NCAA championship

1992   Hill's Blue Devils celebrate a 35-2 season; Hill fires the pass to Christian Laettner that allows Duke to beat Kentucky in one of the most exciting college basketball games ever; Duke goes on to beat Michigan for its second straight NCAA championship

1993   Hill is named nation's best defensive collegiate player but Duke is upset in the second round of the NCAA tournament

1994   Hill leads Duke to its fourth NCAA championship game in five years; Hill is the third pick in the NBA draft, selected by the Detroit Pistons; he signs an eight-year contract worth $45 million and inks other promotional deals that are worth $5 million per year

1995   Hill becomes the only rookie to be the leading vote getter in the NBA All-Star Game; he and Jason Kidd are named Rookies of the Year; Hill is named to the All-Rookie team

1996   As a member of the U.S. Men's Basketball Team, Hill helps lead the squad to a gold medal in the 1996 Atlanta Summer Olympics; he also leads all NBA players in All-Star voting.

1997   Hill increases his scoring average to over 21 points per game, is again named to the All-Star team, and ranks in the top 20 in four important NBA statistical categories: scoring (12th), rebounding (18th), assists (12th), and steals (16th).

SUGGESTIONS FOR FURTHER READING

Geffner, Michael, P., "The Name of the Father." *Sporting News*, January, 16, 1995

Hill, Grant. *Change the Game.* New York: Warner Books, 1996

Junod, Tom, "The Savior." *Gentlemen's Quarterly*, April, 1995

Lupica, Mike, "Amazing Grace." *Esquire*, February, 1995

Plummer, William, "Shooting Star." *People Weekly*, January 23, 1995

Wolff, Alexander, "The Son is Shining." *Sports Illustrated*, February 1, 1993

ABOUT THE AUTHOR

Daniel Bial is an editor, literary agent, and book packager. He was an editor at HarperCollins Publishers for 10 years where he worked on hundreds of titles, including the autobiographies of Hank Aaron and Tom Landry. He lives in New York City with his wife, Abby, daughter, Miriam, and two cats.

PICTURE CREDITS:

AP/Wide World: pp. 2, 8,11, 20, 28, 32, 36, 42, 44, 47, 48, 52, 54, 58; courtesy, Yale University, Department of Athletics: 14; UPI/Bettmann: 16,19; Reston Times 23, 24; Eric Miller—Reuters/Archive Photos: 39.

INDEX